# WHAT IS THE SUN?

## BRIDGET HEOS

Britannica®
Educational Publishing

IN ASSOCIATION WITH

ROSEN
EDUCATIONAL SERVICES

Published in 2015 by Britannica Educational Publishing (a trademark of Encyclopædia Britannica, Inc.) in association with The Rosen Publishing Group, Inc.
29 East 21st Street, New York, NY 10010

Distributed exclusively by Rosen Publishing.
To see additional Britannica Educational Publishing titles, go to rosenpublishing.com.

First Edition

**Britannica Educational Publishing**
J.E. Luebering: Director, Core Reference Group
Mary Rose McCudden, Britannica Student Encyclopedia

**Rosen Publishing**
Hope Lourie Killcoyne: Executive Editor
Nelson Sá: Art Director
Nicole Russo: Designer
Cindy Reiman: Photography Manager
Amy Feinberg: Photo Researcher

**Cataloging-in-Publication Data**

Heos, Bridget, author.
What is the Sun?/Bridget Heos.
    pages cm. — (Let's find out! Space)
Includes bibliographical references and index.
ISBN 978-1-62275-461-8 (library bound) — ISBN 978-1-62275-463-2 (pbk.) — ISBN 978-1-62275-464-9 (6-pack)
1. Sun — Juvenile literature. 2. Stars — Juvenile literature. I. Title.
QB521.5.H46 2015
523.7 — dc23

2014003910

*Manufactured in the United States of America*

# CONTENTS

# Overview

The Sun warms Earth and lights our days, but what is a sun? A sun is a star that is the center of a solar system. All suns are stars, but not all stars are suns because some stars exist without planets surrounding them.

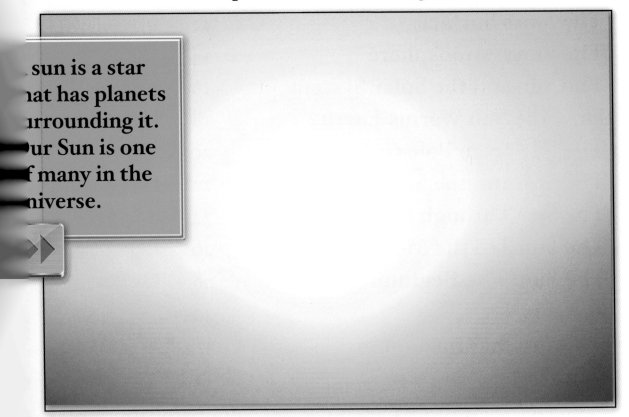

sun is a star
that has planets
surrounding it.
Our Sun is one
of many in the
universe.

A star is a hot sphere of gases that gives off energy in the form of light and heat. Our Sun is one of many stars in the universe. Scientists have theorized that there are at least 100 billion galaxies in the universe. In our galaxy alone (the Milky Way), there are about 200 billion stars.

**THINK ABOUT IT**
Most solar systems have two or more stars. What would a sunrise be like with two suns?

Only a few thousand stars (all from our own galaxy) are visible to the naked eye. The Andromeda galaxy can also be seen, but it appears like a single star.

# Star Light, Star Bright

Stars vary in color from blue to yellow to red. Blue stars are hotter than red stars, and yellow stars are in the midrange. Hotter stars tend to be brighter than cooler stars. However, the size of a star also affects the brightness.

Red giants and supergiant stars are relatively

Proxima Centauri, shown here through the Hubble Space Telescope, is our closest neighboring star. Because it is small and dim, it is invisible to the naked eye.

cool but bright because of their size. (The diameter of a supergiant can be 100 times that of the Sun.) In contrast, a white dwarf is hot but dim because it is small. Our Sun, a yellow star, is in the midrange of size and brightness.

**THINK ABOUT IT**
HP 56948, a star 200 light-years away from Earth, has the same mass, temperature, and chemical composition as our Sun. Scientists wonder if it has a planet in its solar system similar to Earth. What might this other Earth be like?

All stars are big and hot, but some are bigger or hotter than others. Our Sun is in the average range of heat and size.

# NEIGHBORS AND TWINS

The three closest stars to the Sun are known as Alpha Centauri. Alpha Centauri A is a yellow star. Alpha Centauri B is redder. They orbit each other and together are the fourth-brightest star in Earth's sky. A red dwarf star called Proxima Centauri orbits both stars. At 4.2 light-years away, it is the

A star's brightness in the night sky depends on its closeness to Earth, its size, and its heat. Sirius is the brightest star in the night sky.

closest star to Earth. These stars are not thought to be orbited by planets that support life.

A star that has the same mass, temperature, and chemical composition as the Sun is HP 56948. It is 200 light-years away. Scientists wonder if it has a planet in its solar system similar to Earth. If so, it might be home to similar life-forms.

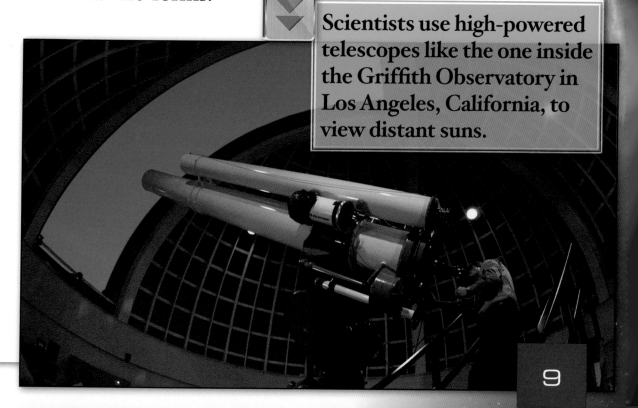

Scientists use high-powered telescopes like the one inside the Griffith Observatory in Los Angeles, California, to view distant suns.

# THE SUN'S CORE

Let's look more closely at our Sun. Its core consists mostly of the gases hydrogen and helium. Its core is very hot, probably reaching about 28,080,000°F (15,600,000°C). Hydrogen is packed in tightly at the core, creating a density 150 times greater than water density. Have you ever dived deep into a

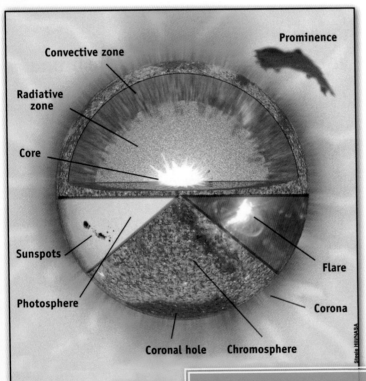

Convective zone

Radiative zone

Core

Sunspots

Photosphere

Coronal hole

Prominence

Flare

Corona

Chromosphere

Sissie Hill/NASA

This diagram shows the parts of the Sun.

swimming pool and felt your ears hurt? That was because of the water pressure. The Sun's pressure is much greater than that! The pressure causes hydrogen atoms to fuse with each other, changing into helium. This process releases huge amounts of energy: the Sun's heat and light.

**Density** is the quantity of something, such as molecules, per unit volume, unit area, or unit length.

When swimming, one often notices how powerful the pressure of water can be. The pressure present in the Sun's core is 100 billion times that of the atmospheric pressure on Earth. ▶▶

# THE SUN'S SURFACE

The energy created in the Sun's core radiates through its surface, which also consists of gas. This means that even if the Sun were not so hot, you could not stand on it. The Sun's surface is, of course, very hot, though not as hot as its core. The surface temperature is about 10,000° F (6,000° C).

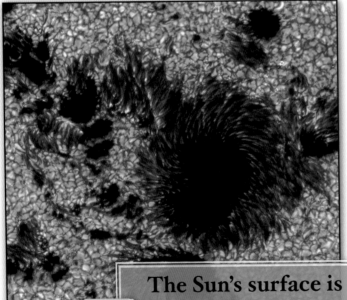

The surface emits most of the light and heat that reach Earth. Sometimes cooler, darker patches

The Sun's surface is not as hot as its core, but it still reaches temperatures of 10,000°F (6,000°C). Sunspots, shown here, sometimes appear on the surface.

called sunspots appear on the surface. They appear and disappear in 11-year cycles.

Like Earth, the Sun rotates. Because its surface is made of gas, the entire Sun does not rotate at the same speed. Its equator rotates every 25 days. At the poles, it rotates every 36 days.

The Sun rotates at different speeds, moving faster at the equator and slower toward the poles. This is called differential rotation.

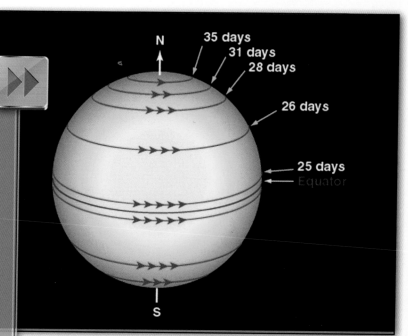

# THE SUN'S ATMOSPHERE

Layers of gases, called an **atmosphere**, surround the Sun. The surface is the first layer of the Sun's atmosphere. This layer is called the photosphere. The next layer is called the chromosphere. It is visible as a thin reddish ring around the edge of the Sun during total solar eclipses.

The part of the Sun that can be seen through a filtered telescope is the photosphere. (The Sun should never be viewed directly; it can cause eye damage.)

The outer atmosphere is called the corona. It is visible as a white halo during a solar eclipse. The Sun's hot corona (reaching 3,600,000°F (2,000,000°C) shoots out particles that carry an electric charge. The stream of particles is called the solar wind. The wind moves out through the solar system at about 250 miles (400 kilometers) per second. On Earth, these solar winds can cause colorful bands of light called auroras to appear in the far northern and southern skies.

An **atmosphere** is a layer of gases surrounding a heavenly body, such as a planet or sun.

Auroras can be viewed from Earth in the far north and south. They are known as the southern lights, shown here, and the northern lights.

# THE SUN AND THE SOLAR SYSTEM

Planets orbit a sun because of its strong gravitational pull. The more mass an object has, the greater its gravitational pull. Our Sun contains more than 99 percent of the mass contained in the entire solar system.

Planets surround a sun because of its strong gravitational pull. Eight planets and several dwarf planets orbit our Sun.

The four planets closest to the Sun have solid surfaces. Mercury is closest, orbiting at a distance of 36 million miles (58 million kilometers). For this reason, temperatures on Mercury can exceed 800°F (430°C) during the day.

The four outer planets consist of liquid and gas. The largest of these "gas giants" is Jupiter. Like the Sun, it is made up of hydrogen and helium. If Jupiter were 80 times larger, it would be massive enough to create the energy needed to be a star. As it is, Jupiter lies at the center of dozens of orbiting moons.

## THINK ABOUT IT

Some "stars" in the night sky are not stars at all but the planets Mercury, Mars, Venus, Saturn, and Jupiter. From some of these same planets, Earth appears like a star.

Because of its proximity to Earth, Jupiter is as bright in the night sky as a star. Though it is the largest planet, Jupiter is too small to be a star.

# How the Sun Warms Earth

Earth orbits the Sun at a distance of about 93 million miles (150 million kilometers). The Sun is the source of virtually all Earth's energy. But if Earth relied on the Sun's heat alone, the average temperature would be 0°F (-18°C), too cold for most living things.

In reality, Earth is a balmy 58°F (14°C) on average. This is because of

The Sun is very hot. But if Earth relied on the Sun's heat alone, our planet would be a frozen ball of ice.

the greenhouse effect. When the Sun's rays hit Earth, some heat is absorbed. But much of it is reflected back toward space. Some of this heat is trapped by gases in Earth's atmosphere. This also means that Earth stays warm at night.

**THINK ABOUT IT**

Though broiling hot during the day, Mercury's temperature drops to - 300°F (- 180°C) at night. What does Mercury lack that Earth has?

The greenhouse effect explains why Earth has a relatively warm climate. Gases in Earth's atmosphere trap some of the Sun's heat.

# THE SUN FROM POLE TO POLE

The Sun's rays hit Earth directly at the **equator** during two seasons of the year. That means the rays are directed at a small area. Where the rays enter at more of a slant, toward the North and South Poles, the heat from the Sun is spread out over a larger area. Imagine a space heater used to heat one room versus a whole house. A room would get very warm, but a whole house would

Earth's tilt determines where the Sun's rays hit Earth. In this picture, the Sun is shining directly on the Tropic of Capricorn. It is summer in the Southern Hemisphere.

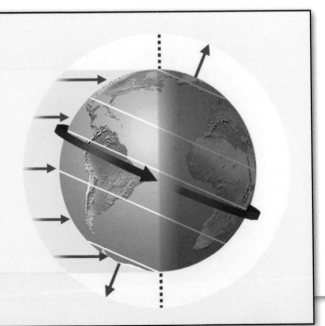

remain pretty cold. The same is true at the equator, where it is always warm, and toward the poles, where it is cold.

Because of Earth's slant, hours of daylight vary widely at the poles. During the summer, the Arctic has 24 hours of sunlight. During the winter, it is plunged into round-the-clock darkness. The same is true of Antarctica, only at opposite times of the year.

The **equator** is an imaginary circle around Earth that is equally distant from the North Pole and the South Pole.

In summertime, the Sun never sets on the Gates of the Arctic National Park and Preserve. This is because the North Pole is tilted toward the Sun.

# THE SUN AND THE SEASONS

Earth tilts by about 23 degrees. In June, July, and August, the Northern Hemisphere is tipped slightly toward the Sun. The Sun hits as far north as the Tropic of Cancer, creating summer in the Northern Hemisphere. June 21 or 22 marks the summer solstice, when the Sun is the farthest north. Winter solstice, when the Sun is farthest south, is on December 21 or 22.

Can you tell which hemisphere this girl lives in? Hint: The picture was taken on July 9. She lives in the Northern Hemisphere, where summer occurs in June, July, and August.

In December, the Sun hits as far south as the Tropic of Capricorn, ushering in summer in the Southern Hemisphere. The summer solstice here is on December 21 or 22, and the winter solstice is on June 21 or 22.

**What about this girl? In which hemisphere does she live? The photo was taken on July 11. In the Southern Hemisphere, winter is in June, July, and August.**

### THINK ABOUT IT

**When it is summer in the Northern Hemisphere, it is winter in the Southern Hemisphere, and vice versa. Why does it stay warm near the equator year-round?**

# THE SUN THROUGH HUMAN HISTORY

Since ancient times, people have been fascinated by the Sun. In England, between 3100 and 1500 BCE, builders arranged some of the pillars at Stonehenge to frame the sunrise during the summer solstice. At around the same time, ancient Egyptians were worshipping Re, the Sun god.

tonehenge in England as built during the Stone ge. Some believe that was built as a sort of oservatory to predict or ark the solstices.

Later, scientists found ways to study the distant Sun. Nicolaus Copernicus argued (in 1543) that Earth orbits the Sun. And in 1686, Isaac Newton published a book explaining how the Sun's gravitational pull causes the planets to orbit it. In modern times, scientists have analyzed the Sun's spectrum to determine what chemicals make up the Sun. They have also sent satellites into space to photograph the Sun and to take measurements.

A **spectrum** is the group of colors, including red, orange, yellow, green, blue, and violet, seen when sunlight passes through a prism.

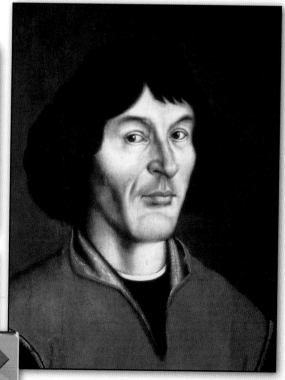

Renaissance mathematician and astronomer Nicolaus Copernicus argued that Earth orbits the Sun, a revolutionary viewpoint at the time.

# The Sun and the Moon

The Moon shines because it reflects sunlight. The extent of the Moon that shows depends on its position in relation to the Sun and Earth. A new Moon occurs when the Moon is between the Sun and Earth. A full Moon happens when Earth is between the Sun and Moon.

During the new Moon, a solar eclipse can occur. Passing in front of the Sun, the Moon appears as a black circle. What looks like a ring of fire appears around the

A full Moon appears when Earth is between the Sun and the Moon. The Moon appears larger when it is near the horizon than it does when it is higher up in the sky.

circle. This ring is the Sun's corona. If Earth completely blocks the Sun, a lunar eclipse can occur. The Moon is then in Earth's shadow. The Moon glows a dim red orange because some sunlight reaches it indirectly.

**THINK ABOUT IT**

If you had no scientific knowledge of the Sun or Moon, what story might you make up to explain what they are?

A lunar eclipse occurs when Earth is directly between the Sun and Moon. Because Earth blocks the sunlight, the Moon receives only indirect sunlight.

# The Sun: The Beginning and End

The Sun is 4.6 billion years old. It formed from a rotating cloud of dust known as a nebula. Gravity caused most of the dust to be pulled toward the center, where it formed the Sun. The remaining dust formed the planets.

The Sun has been a relatively constant ball of energy since its formation. But in another few billion years,

The Sun formed from a cloud of dust known as a nebula. In recent years, NASA telescopes have captured photos of the Orion Nebula.

the Sun will expand into a red giant star. Then it will eject part of its mass into space. What remains of the Sun will be known as a white dwarf star. It will continue to shine for billions of years, even as it gradually cools.

That won't happen for a long, long time. In the meantime, living things will continue to thrive because of the Sun's light and heat.

A **nebula** is a giant cloud of gas or dust in space.

Al₂O₃ dust

SiO Maser

Stellar Surface

Molecular Shells

Pulsation

Outflow

This diagram shows the structure of a pulsating red giant. The star is made up of a molecular shell (inner red layer), a dust shell (outer red layer), and a maser (radiation) shell (red and green speckles).

# GLOSSARY

**galaxy** One of the very large groups of stars and other matter that are found throughout the universe.

**gravity** A force of attraction between bodies that occurs because of their masses.

**lunar eclipse** The total or partial hiding of the Moon by Earth's shadow.

**mass** The quantity of matter in a body.

**orbit** The path taken by one body circling around another body.

**particle** One of the very small parts of matter (as a molecule, atom, or electron).

**pressure** The force exerted over an area by a substance.

**ray** A thin beam of radiant energy, such as light.

**solar eclipse** The total or partial hiding of the Sun by the Moon's shadow.

**solar flare** A sudden, temporary outburst of energy from a small area of the Sun's surface.

**solar system** A star with the group of heavenly bodies that revolve around it, such as planets, moons, asteroids, and comets.

**solar wind** The continuous radiation of charged particles from the Sun's surface.

**sunspot** One of the dark spots that appear from time to time on the Sun's surface and are usually visible only through a telescope.

**universe** All of space and everything in it including stars, planets, and galaxies.

# For More Information

## Books

Aguilar, David. *Planets, Stars, and Galaxies: A Visual Encyclopedia of Our Universe.* New York, NY: National Geographic, 2007.

Fox, Karen, and Nancy Davis. *Older Than the Stars.* Boston, MA: Charlesbridge, 2011.

Jefferis, David. *The Sun.* New York, NY: Crabtree, 2008.

Jemison, Mae, and Dana Meachen Rau. *Exploring Our Sun.* New York, NY: Children's Press, 2013.

Scott, Elaine. *Space, Stars, and the Beginning of Time: What the Hubble Telescope Saw.* New York, NY: Clarion, 2011.

## Websites

Because of the changing nature of Internet links, Rosen Publishing has developed an online list of websites related to the subject of this book. This site is updated regularly. Please use this link to access the list:

http://www.rosenlinks.com/lfo/sun

# INDEX